MW01206506

Welcome to Destiny Roberts Books

🩶 Enjoy the journey with Destiny's Books. 🩶

📖 Thank you for choosing this Destiny activity book! ✨

🌱 Our goal is to inspire, encourage, and uplift children as they learn, grow, and explore the world around them. ☀️

Each page is thoughtfully designed to promote:

🎨 Creativity

💪 Confidence

🧠 Curiosity

Whether it's coloring, solving puzzles, or trying something new, every activity is a small step forward in your child's journey. 🐾

📖 We hope this book brings joy, sparks imagination, and encourages pride in every little accomplishment along the way. ⭐

🚀 The Fun Doesn't Stop Here!

✍️ We're busy creating even more exciting workbooks to keep young minds active and inspired all year long! ✨

◎ Coming Summer 2025:

🦕 Dino Discovery Days

🐘 Jungle Adventures

🚗 Vroom! Cars & Trucks Workbook

🦈 Under the Sea Explorers

🌵 Desert Animal Activity Book

Because big imaginations deserve big adventures. 💥📚

For the dads who protect us, play with us, and inspire us every single day. You're our hero, and this book is for you.

This Book belongs to :

_____

Table of Contents

Coloring Pages

9

10

11

12

13

14

15

16

17

18

Maze 1

Maze 2

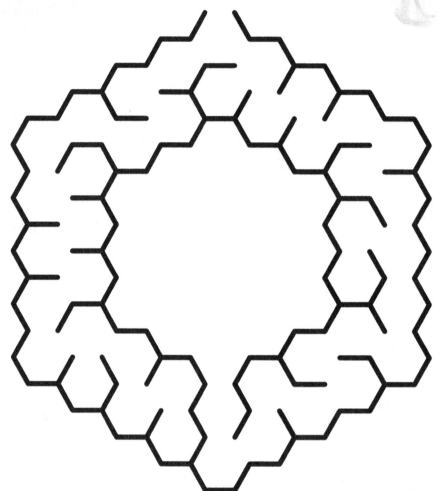

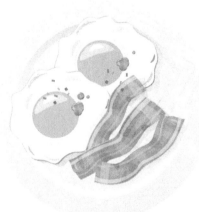

21

Maze 3

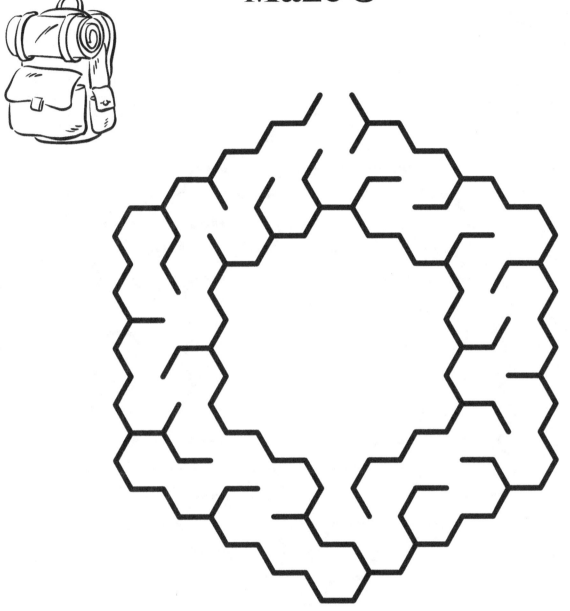

Maze 4

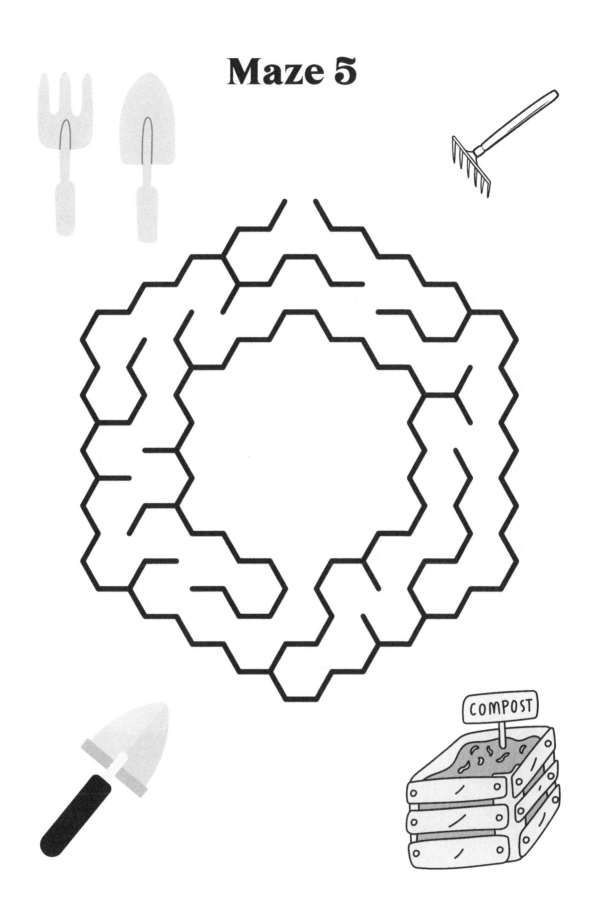

Maze 6

Maze 7

Maze 8

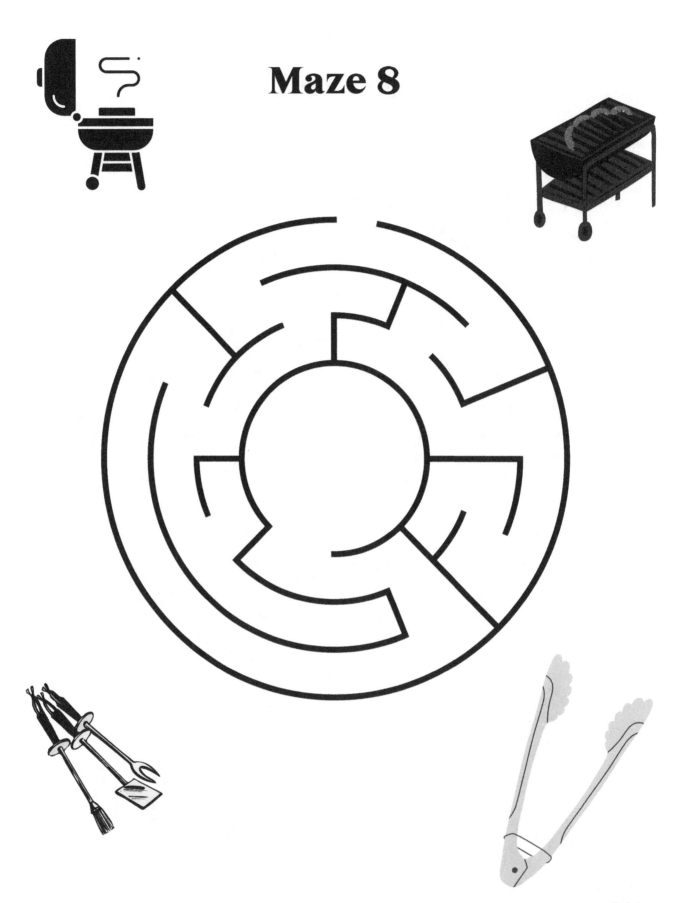

Maze 9

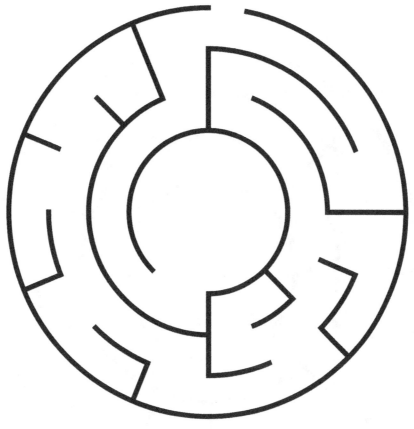

Maze 10

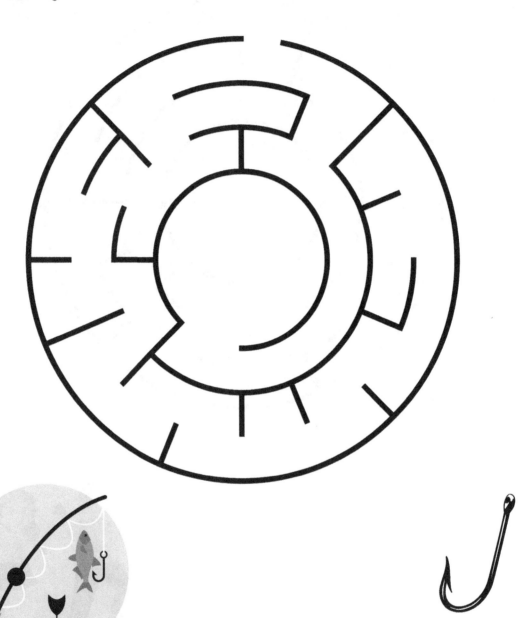

Maze 11

Maze 12

Maze 13

Maze 14

Maze 15

Bonus Section
Drawing

Draw It: Draw a picture when you or one of your siblings tried to dress up like your dad.

Draw It: Draw a picture of a time you and your family laughed so hard at your dad because of what he did.

Draw It: Draw about a camping trip or outing you and your family took with your dad.

Draw It: Draw a picture of your dad playing his favorite sport or doing his favorite activity.

39

Draw It: Draw a picture of you and your family spending quality time without electronics together. What will you do?

40

Bonus Section
Writing

Write the thing you like most about your dad.

Write your dad a sentence that tells him something special about you.

Write a sentence that tells your dad what makes you happy about your family.

Write your dad a sentence why you want to be just like him.

Write a sentence telling your dad how much you love him.

Bonus

Design

Design: a talent show in honor of dads.

Design: a car that you know your dad will absolutely love.

49

Design: the perfect career or job your dad will absolutely love to have.

50

Design: a car or truck show for your dad.

51

Design: a picture of what a great camping trip looks like with your dad.

52

Maze
Solutions

Maze 1

Maze 2

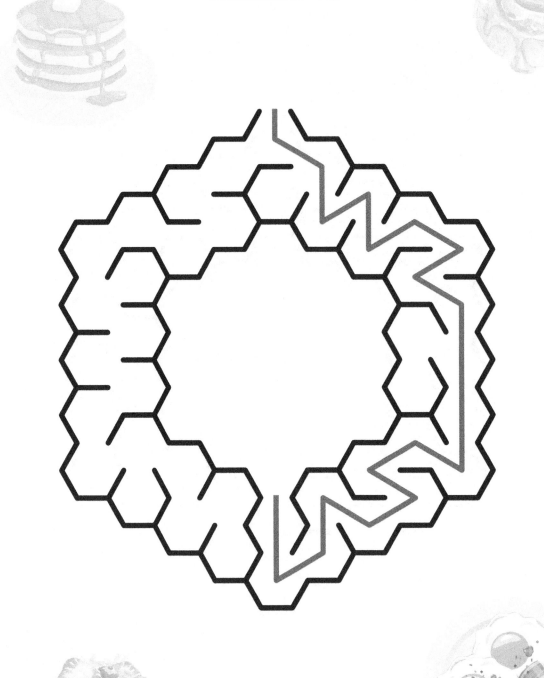

Maze 3

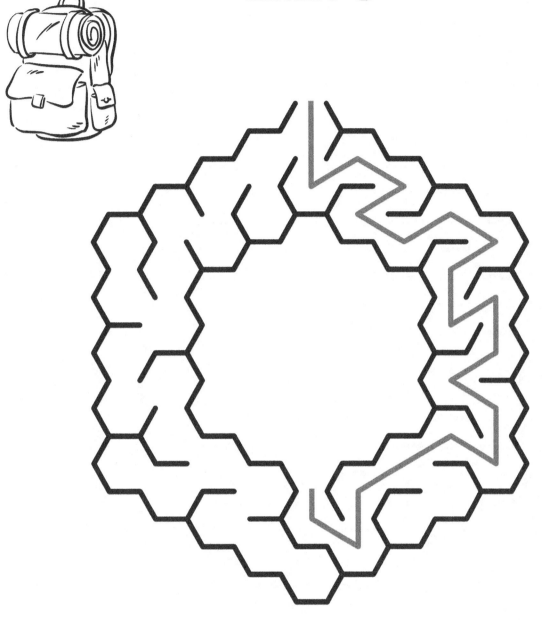

Maze 4

Maze 5

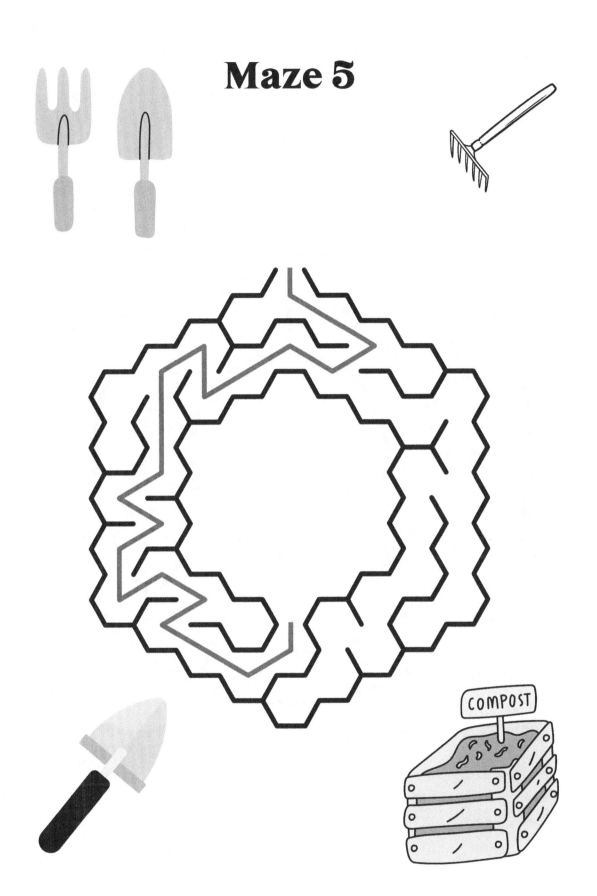

Maze 6

Maze 7

Maze 8

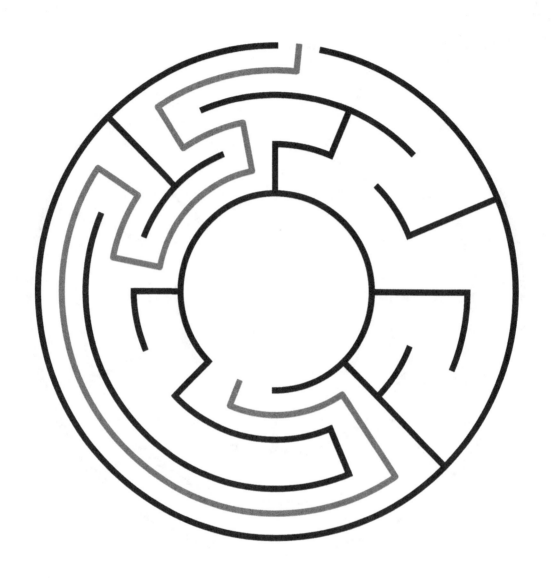

Maze 9

Maze 10

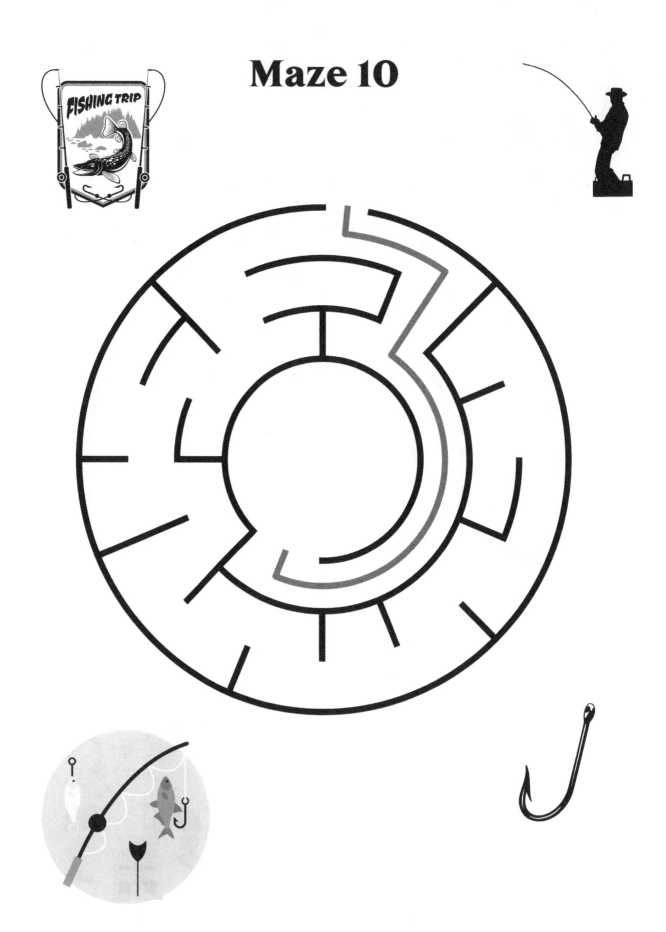

Maze 11

Maze 12

Maze 13

Maze 14

Maze 15

Made in United States
North Haven, CT
03 June 2025

69487307R00037